STRANGE SCIENCE AND EXPLOSIVE EXPERIMENTS

SHATTERING
SOUNDS

WRITTEN BY MIKE CLARK

PowerKiDS
press™

Published in 2018 by
The Rosen Publishing Group, Inc.
29 East 21st Street, New York, NY 10010

Cataloging-in-Publication Data
Names: Clark, Mike.
Title: Shattering sounds / Mike Clark.
Description: New York : PowerKids Press, 2018. | Series: Strange
    science and explosive experiments | Includes index.
Identifiers: ISBN 9781538323687 (pbk.) | ISBN 9781538322727
    (library bound) | ISBN 9781538323694 (6 pack)
Subjects: LCSH: Sound--Experiments--Juvenile literature. |
    Science projects--Juvenile literature.
Classification: LCC QC225.5 C53 2018 | DDC 534.078--dc23

Written by: Mike Clark
Edited by: Charlie Ogden
Designed by: Matt Rumbelow

Photo credits: Abbreviations: l-left, r-right, b-bottom, t-top, c-center, m-middle. All images
courtesy of Shutterstock, unless otherwise specified. With thanks to 2 – Roman Voloshyn.
4 - ChiccoDodiFC. 5 - Joseph Sohm. 6 - Photology1971. 7: t - CamPot; tm - Jacob Lund;
mb - Sunny studio; b - Triff. 8: tr - Vladimir Arndt; ml - IB Photography; mc - artproem; mr -
Dimedrol68; bl - tanuha2001; br - OmniArt. 9 - Love the wind. 10: c - focal point; b - Africa
Studio. 11: bg - LuckyImages; bl - eurobanks. 12: m - horiyan; bl - Zerbor; br - stuart.ford.
13 - Africa Studio. 14: b - SvetaZi. 15: bg - Lradcorporation / wikipedia; U.S. Navy / wikipedia.
16 bl - InesBazdar. 17 - Mihai Simonia. 18: t - saknakorn; bl - Coprid; br - IB Photography.
19 - Tom Wang. 21: bg - Ivan Kuzmin. bl - Simon Hinkley & Ken Walker, Museum Victoria /
wikipedia. 22: t - MANDY GODBEHEAR; b - Geza Farkas. 23: t - iurii; bl - Muinsuskaitseamet.
24 - Maxx-Studio. 25: tr - Red On, bl - Consumer Reports. 26: Harris & Ewing / wikipedia.
27: t - Everett Collection; b - Gilbert H. Grosvenor Collection, Prints and Photographs Division,
Library of Congress / wikipedia. 28 - Wellcome Library, London. 29: t - Wellcome Library,
London; b1 - Wesley Silva de Souza, b2 - Alex Staroseltsev. r.

Manufactured in China

CPSIA Compliance Information: Batch BW18PK: For Further Information contact
Rosen Publishing, New York, New York at 1-800-237-9932.

CONTENTS

Words that appear like this can be found in the glossary on page 31.

Simply Sound

Sound is made when atoms **vibrate**. Atoms are tiny particles that make up matter. Matter is anything that has weight or takes up space. For example, wood is a type of matter. When you knock on a wooden door, you cause the atoms in the wood to vibrate and make a knocking sound.

When one atom vibrates, it causes the one next to it to vibrate and so on. You can think about it like a human wave. When one person stands, raises their arms and sits down, the person next to them will do the same thing. When lots of people do this in a row, it creates a wave in the crowd. Sound is made when a wave of vibrations enters your ears and hits your **eardrum**.

CROWD PERFORMING A WAVE

Wacky Waves

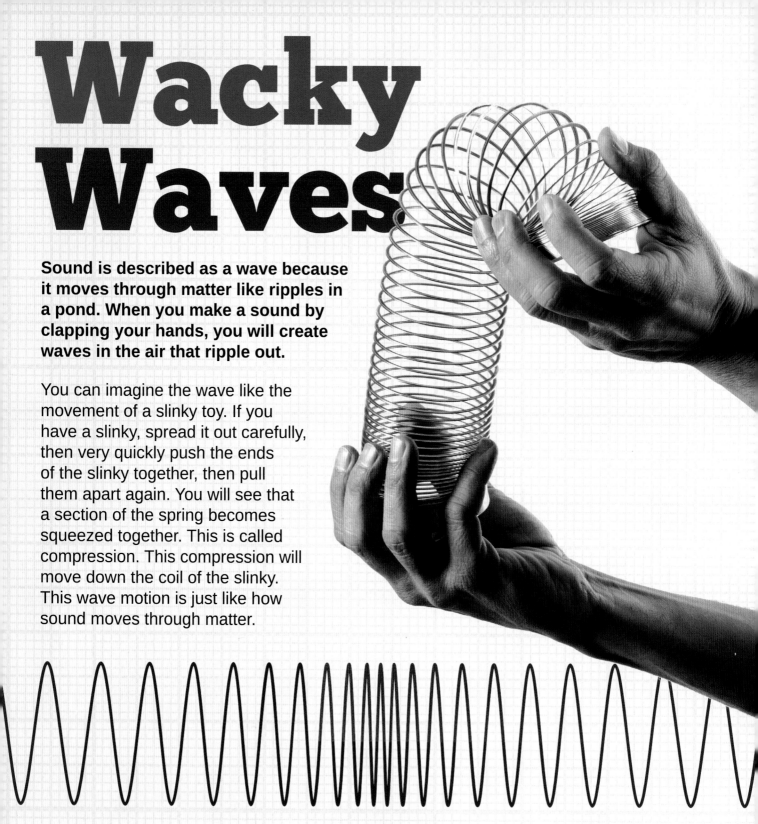

Sound is described as a wave because it moves through matter like ripples in a pond. When you make a sound by clapping your hands, you will create waves in the air that ripple out.

You can imagine the wave like the movement of a slinky toy. If you have a slinky, spread it out carefully, then very quickly push the ends of the slinky together, then pull them apart again. You will see that a section of the spring becomes squeezed together. This is called compression. This compression will move down the coil of the slinky. This wave motion is just like how sound moves through matter.

COMPRESSION

Sound moves through solid matter, like metal, better than it does through liquid matter, like water. This is because the atoms in solids are closer together so they can pass on the vibrations much faster.

Sound travels slowest through gas because atoms in gas are farther apart. In space, however, sound cannot travel at all because there is no air, which means there is no matter for the sound to vibrate through.

SOLID

LIQUID

AIR

SPACE

Dancing Drum

Sound waves in air will travel into objects and make them vibrate. Sometimes loud music can make objects vibrate. To see this effect for yourself, all you will need is:

SPEAKER

SCISSORS

SALT

BALLOON

PLASTIC TUB

A DEVICE THAT CAN CONNECT TO THE SPEAKERS

Step 1)

Using your scissors, cut off the opening section of the balloon and stretch it over the plastic tub to make a drum.

Step 2)

Sprinkle about a teaspoon of salt over the top of the drum.

Step 3)

Position a speaker close to your drum. Now play loud music through it and watch the salt dance.

You should find that the salt jumps about and moves along the surface of your drum.
The salt moves because the vibrations made by the speaker travel through the air and then through the drum, making the skin over the drum shake. This causes the salt on top to bounce.

Piercing Pitch and Volatile Volume

All sound waves have a pitch and a volume. Pitch describes the frequency of the sound wave. Frequency is how close together each sound wave is. A low-pitched sound, such as the sound made by a bass drum, has a lower frequency than a high-pitched sound like that of a penny whistle. This means the sound waves coming from a bass drum are farther apart than those in a penny whistle. The frequency of sound waves is measured in hertz (Hz).

Humans can hear sound waves traveling at a frequency between 20 and 20,000 Hz. Dogs can hear between 67 and 45,000 Hz. **Dog whistles** make a sound above 23,000 Hz. Dogs are able to hear sounds at this frequency but humans are not.

Volume is how loud a sound is. Volume is determined by the height of a sound wave. Loud sounds have taller sound waves than quieter sounds. For example, if you tap the same drum once, and then again much harder, you will notice that the pitch will be the same, but the sound will be much louder the second time.

0 Hz   20   20 000

Infra sound   Audible   Ultra sound
               frequencies

Groovy Guitar

Musical instruments can give a wide range of high and low-pitched sounds. A guitar has many strings that all make sounds at a slightly different pitch. The thinnest string of a guitar has the highest pitch and the thickest has the lowest pitch.

A shorter string also makes the pitch higher. Guitarists can change the length of the string by pressing down on one of the strings with their fingers. To test this effect out for yourself all you will need is:

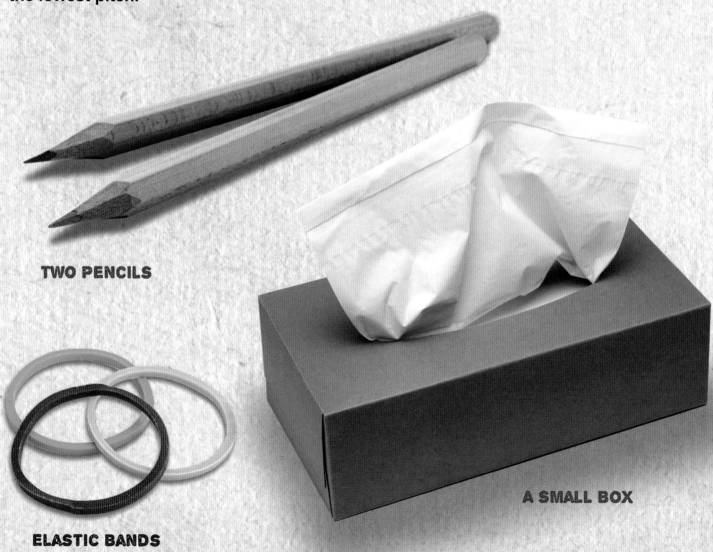

TWO PENCILS

A SMALL BOX

ELASTIC BANDS

Stretch the elastic bands over the empty box.

Step 2)

Slide one pencil under the elastic bands on the left side and the other on the right side. This is so that the vibrations do not get absorbed into the box right away.

Step 3)

Pluck the rubber bands. Listen to the pitch given out. Now move one pencil closer to the other pencil. Pluck again and you should hear that the pitch of the sound becomes higher.

A GUITARIST CHANGING THE PITCH OF THE GUITAR'S SOUND BY PRESSING DOWN THE STRINGS

Splitting Speakers

Speakers turn pulses of electricity into sound. A speaker has three main parts. A magnet, a coil of wire and a cone. The cone is attached to the coil of wire and the coil of wire is placed in front of the magnet.

When electricity is passed through the coil of wire, it is pushed away from the magnet.

The stronger the current of electricity running along the wire, the farther the coil of wire will move away from the magnet. This causes the cone, which is attached to the coil of wire, to move back and forth with it. As the cone moves back and forth, it pushes the air forward very quickly. This push creates vibrations in the air, which make sound waves.

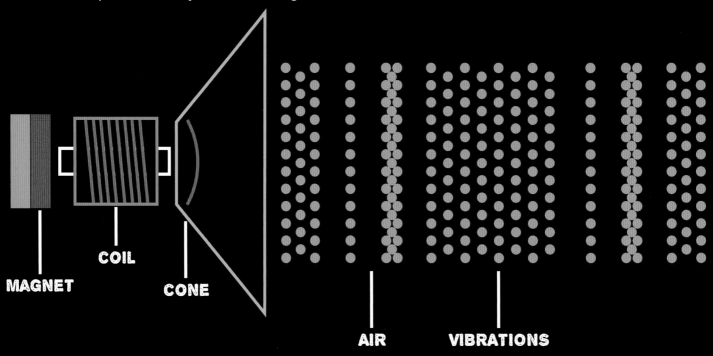

MAGNET COIL CONE

AIR VIBRATIONS

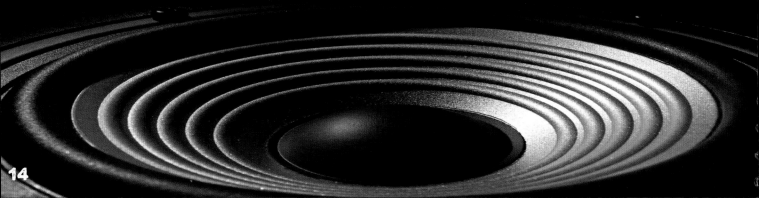

Speakers can be very powerful. For example, a speaker called a Long Range Acoustic Device (LRAD) can be used as a weapon because it is able to vibrate the insides of your ears so harshly that it begins to hurt. This kind of weapon is called a sonic weapon.

Super Speech

The human voice is much more complicated than an electronic speaker. The sounds we make when speaking or singing are a result of our nose, mouth, lungs and thin layers of tissue in our throat called vocal folds, all working together. The vocal folds are positioned in your **trachea**.

The vocal folds are used to change the pitch of the sound you make. As you speak, you blow air out of your lungs, which then passes through the vocal folds. The vocal folds change the size of the opening to your lungs as you speak. A narrower opening will make the pitch of your voice higher and a wider opening will make it lower.

VOCAL FOLDS

TRACHEA

Parts of your nose and mouth also help create different sounds. Pinch your nose and try saying, "Go get a bigger egg." Now say, "Mama made lemon jam." The first sentence is not affected at all but the second sentence probably sounds very different. This is because we use our noses to make an "M" sound.

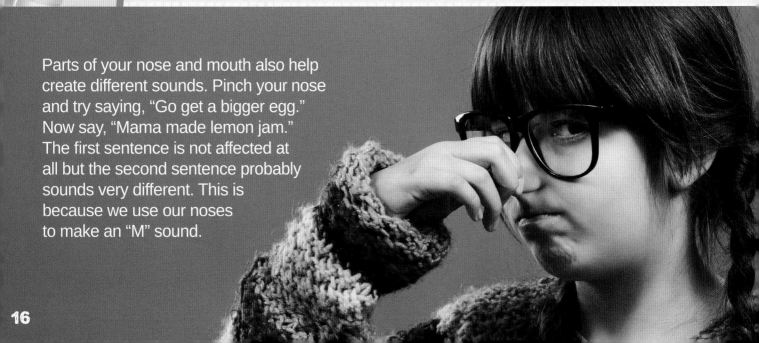

The volume of our voice is controlled by our lungs. The faster the air is pushed out, the louder your voice will be. We measure the volume of sounds in decibels. Decibels measure the strength of the vibrations in a sound wave. The loudest recorded scream in the world belongs to Jill Drake, a teacher from the U.K., who can scream as loud as 129 decibels. This is even louder than thunder, which is usually about 120 decibels.

Mighty Megaphone

You can make your voice even louder by using a megaphone. Megaphones have been used for years, especially by film directors who want to be heard by all their crew across the film set. To create your own megaphone, all you need is:

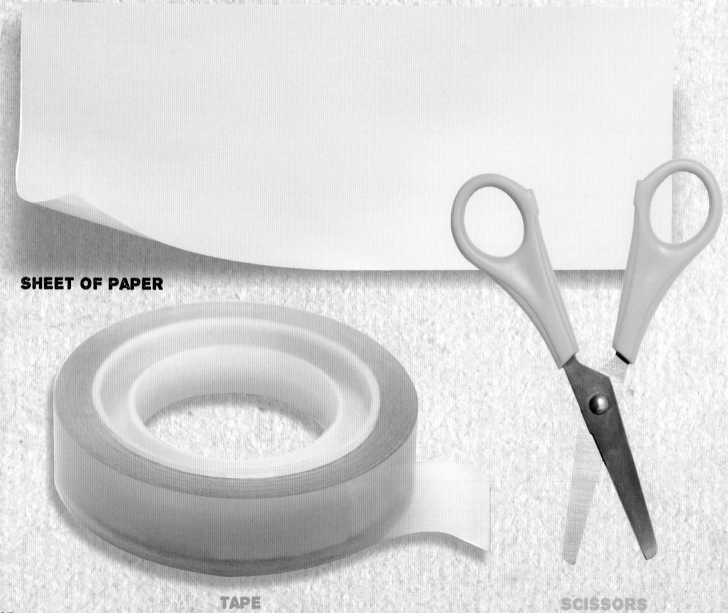

SHEET OF PAPER

TAPE

SCISSORS

Step 1)

Roll up the sheet of paper into a cone shape and tape it in place.

Step 2)

Cut along the end of either side of the cone to leave a flat edge.

Step 3)

Get a friend to stand across the room from you. Speak normally and then speak through the megaphone at the same volume. Your voice should be easier to hear with the megaphone.

The megaphone makes your voice louder by focusing the sound waves in one direction. When you speak, the vibrations are pushed through a small opening and then out in the direction the megaphone is pointed.

Humming Hearing

We sense sound through our ears. Our ears absorb sound waves and send this information to the brain. Like a drum, ears have a thin layer of skin that vibrates back and forth when sound waves hit it. This is called the eardrum. As the eardrum moves back and forth, it moves three tiny bones called the ossicles. When these three bones are moved, they send information about the vibrations to the brain in the form of electrical signals. The brain turns the information into sound.

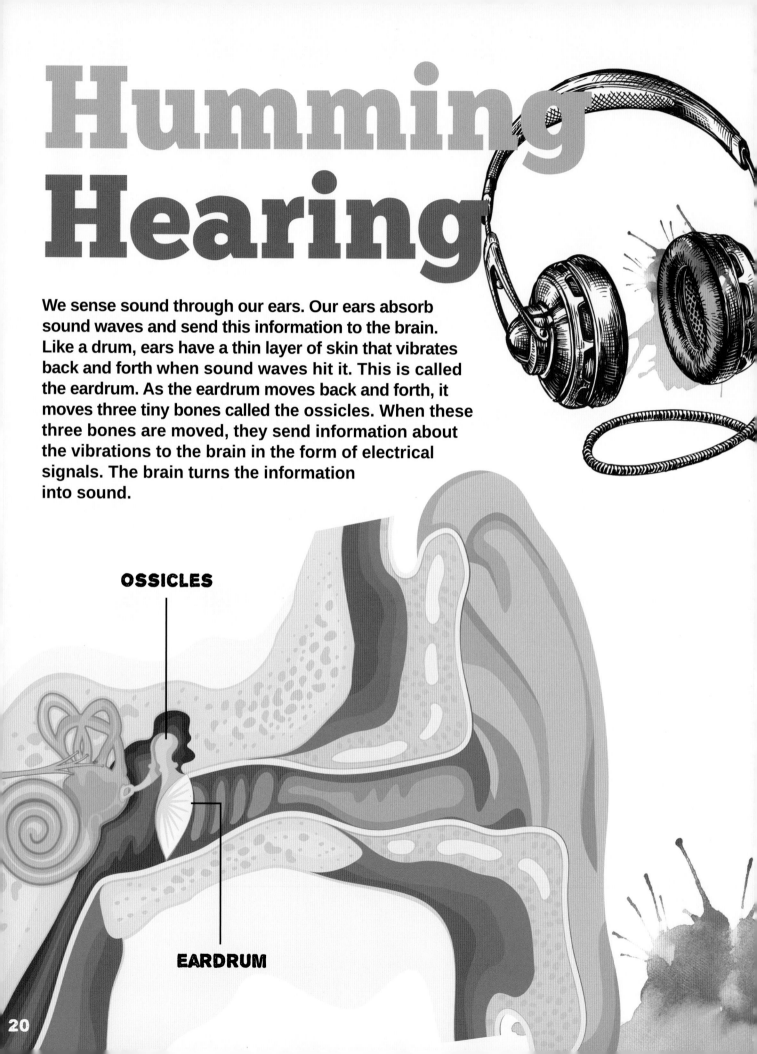

OSSICLES

EARDRUM

Our hearing is measured by the amount of hertz we can hear. Hertz is the frequency of sound. The higher the number, the higher the pitch of the sound. A human can hear between 20 and 20,000 Hz but this is a small hearing range compared to other animals. Many bats can hear up to 200,000 Hz. But the best hearing of all belongs to an insect called the greater wax moth. It can hear sounds of up to 300,000 Hz.

FRUIT BAT

THE GREATER
WAX MOTH

Extreme Echoes

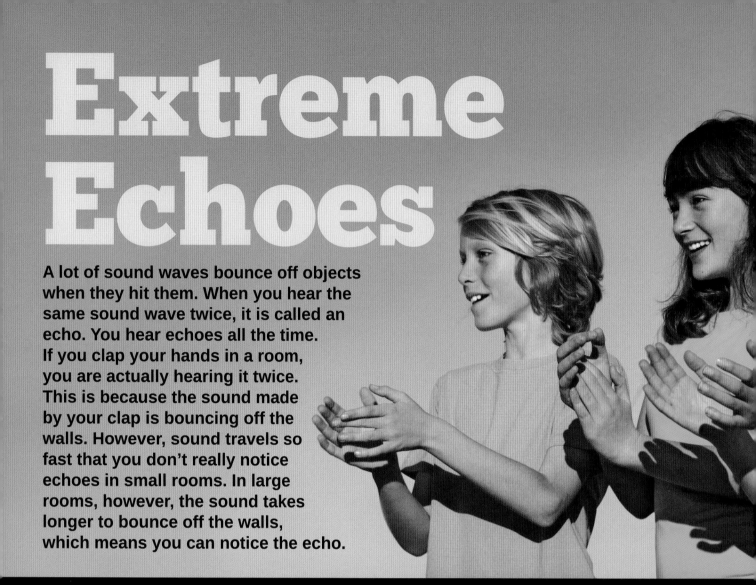

A lot of sound waves bounce off objects when they hit them. When you hear the same sound wave twice, it is called an echo. You hear echoes all the time. If you clap your hands in a room, you are actually hearing it twice. This is because the sound made by your clap is bouncing off the walls. However, sound travels so fast that you don't really notice echoes in small rooms. In large rooms, however, the sound takes longer to bounce off the walls, which means you can notice the echo.

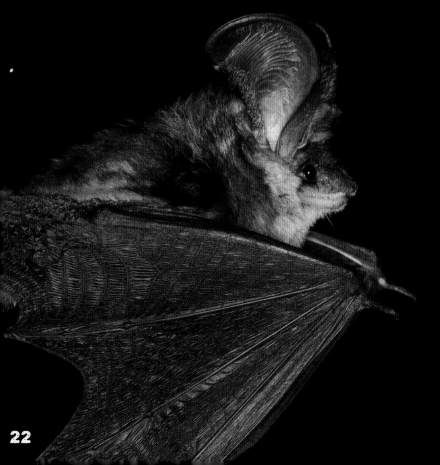

Some animals can work out where something is by listening for the echo of a sound. The brown long-eared bat uses echoes to find food. Bats fly around at night looking for insects, but, because there is no light at night, the bats have to use sound to find food. They send out a very high-pitched call and listen for the echo with their big ears. When they hear the echo of their call bouncing off an insect, they can work out where that insect is hiding. This is called echolocation.

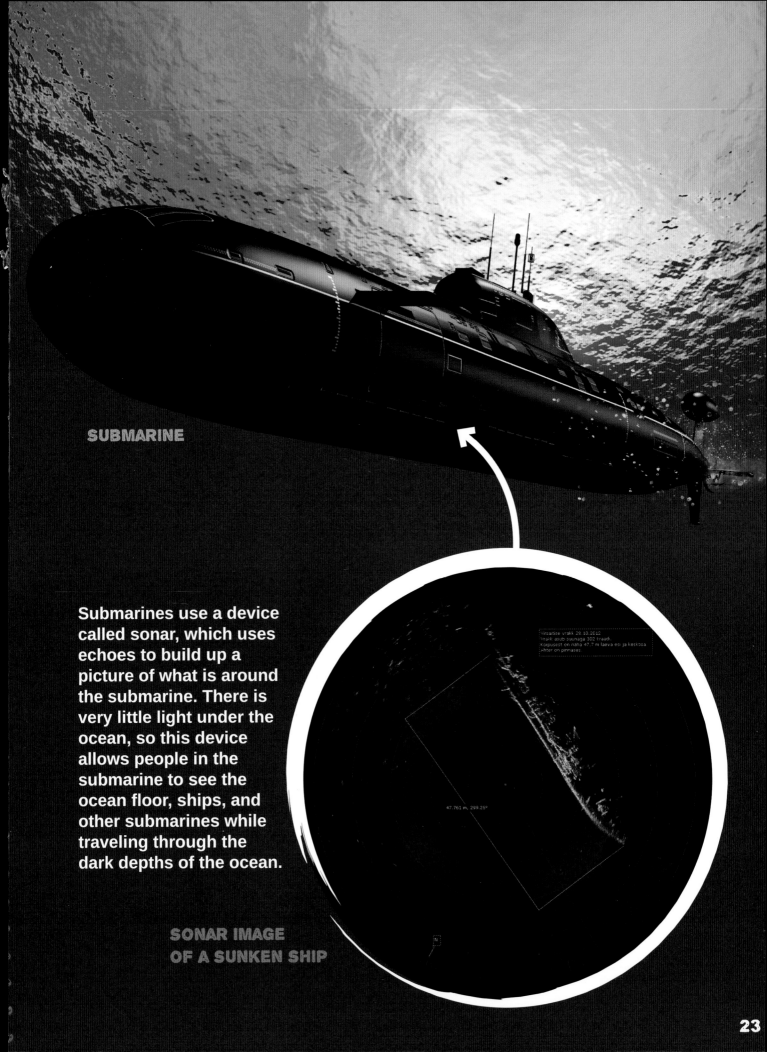

SUBMARINE

Submarines use a device called sonar, which uses echoes to build up a picture of what is around the submarine. There is very little light under the ocean, so this device allows people in the submarine to see the ocean floor, ships, and other submarines while traveling through the dark depths of the ocean.

SONAR IMAGE
OF A SUNKEN SHIP

Shuddering Silence

There is always sound going on around us. We just don't notice it because it's always there. Even when your house is really quiet, your fridge will be humming and your TV will be buzzing, even when it's turned off. You might even be able to hear the hum of traffic outside. However, there are rooms that are designed to be completely silent. These rooms are called anechoic chambers. Anechoic is **Latin** for "no echo." If you sat in one of these rooms by yourself, it would be so quiet that you would be able to hear your own heartbeat.

CLOSE-UP OF A WALL IN AN ANECHOIC CHAMBER

Anechoic chambers have spiky walls, which are designed to absorb sound. Low-pitched sounds bounce off the slanted edges of the spikes, which causes the sound wave to bounce upwards and hit the spike above it. The sound waves then bounce back and forth between the two spikes, traveling farther into the wall until it is absorbed. High-pitched sounds get absorbed right away into the soft foam material that the spikes are made of.

TESTING A PAIR OF HEADPHONES IN AN ANECHOIC CHAMBER

These rooms are used to test sound equipment like speakers or headphones. However, many people claim that when you sit in these rooms, the silence is so unnatural that it can drive you mad. A few have even claimed to have experienced sound **hallucinations** inside these rooms, hearing voices and even swarms of bees!

Shocking Scientists

Alexander Graham Bell

Date of Birth: Mar, 3 1847

Date of Death: Aug, 2 1922

Place of Birth: Scotland

Hobbies: Making dogs talk and inventing the telephone.

Alexander Graham Bell was a scientist interested in sound waves who **invented** the first telephone. When he was 12 years old, his mother began to lose her hearing. This made him very interested in studying how we hear and make sound. One of his experiments involved making his dog talk. He trained his dog to growl on demand, then he moved its lips to make almost human-like words.

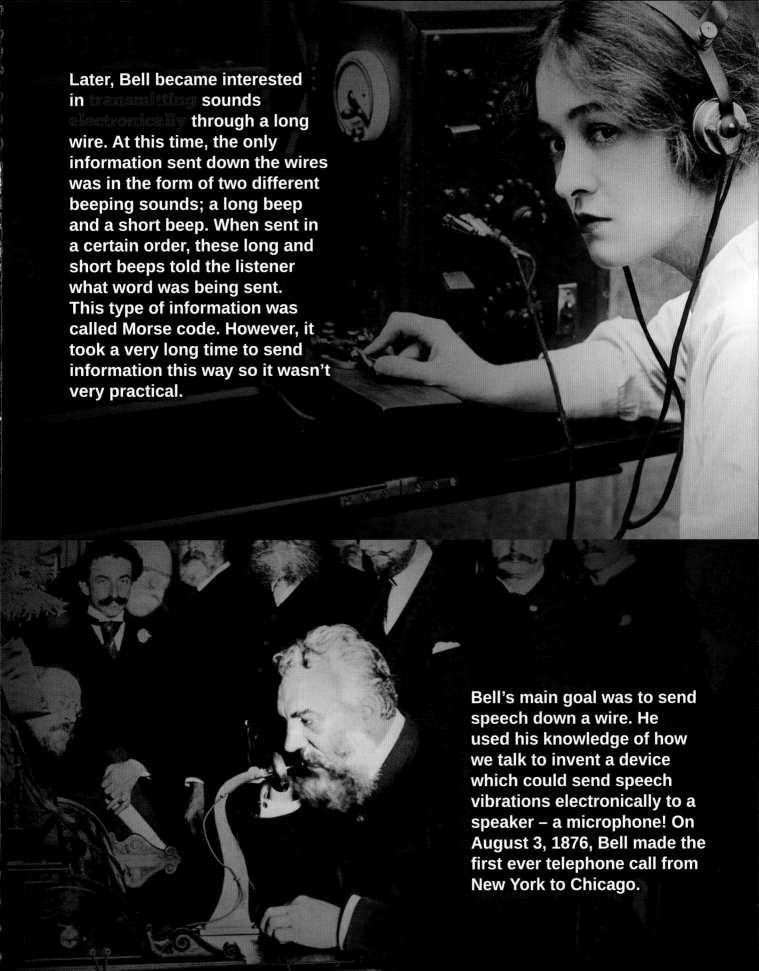

Later, Bell became interested in transmitting sounds electronically through a long wire. At this time, the only information sent down the wires was in the form of two different beeping sounds; a long beep and a short beep. When sent in a certain order, these long and short beeps told the listener what word was being sent. This type of information was called Morse code. However, it took a very long time to send information this way so it wasn't very practical.

Bell's main goal was to send speech down a wire. He used his knowledge of how we talk to invent a device which could send speech vibrations electronically to a speaker – a microphone! On August 3, 1876, Bell made the first ever telephone call from New York to Chicago.

Robert William Boyle

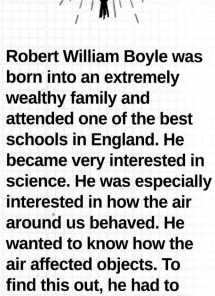

Date of Birth: Jan 25, 1627

Date of Death: Dec 31, 1691

Place of Birth: Ireland

Hobbies: Brushing his long flowing hair and studying how sound moves.

Robert William Boyle was born into an extremely wealthy family and attended one of the best schools in England. He became very interested in science. He was especially interested in how the air around us behaved. He wanted to know how the air affected objects. To find this out, he had to remove air from around the objects. So Boyle invented an air pump that could suck out all the air in a sealed, glass jar to create a **vacuum**.

Boyle began experimenting by placing different objects in the vacuum. One of these objects was a bell. He hung the bell inside of a glass jar and began to pump out the air. While the air was being pumped out, Boyle rang the bell by moving it with a magnet. As the air was pumped out, the sound of the bell became quieter and quieter until it could no longer be heard.

BOYLE'S ORIGINAL DRAWINGS OF HIS EXPERIMENTS USING VACUUMS

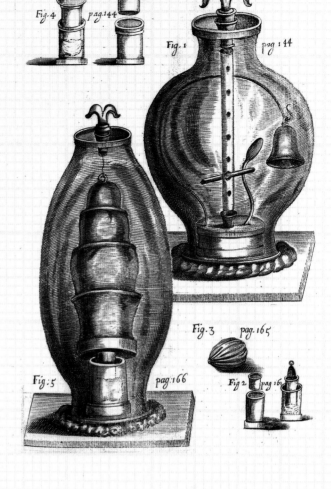

Boyle's experiment proved that sound could only travel through matter. When the air was removed, there was no matter around the bell that could be vibrated. Therefore, the vibrations made by the bell could not travel through the glass jar and out towards Boyle's ears.

A MODERN VERSION OF BOYLE'S EXPERIMENT

QUICK QUIZ

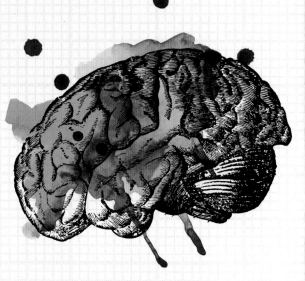

HAVE YOU TAKEN IT ALL IN? TAKE THIS QUICK QUIZ TO TEST YOUR KNOWLEDGE. THE ANSWERS ARE UPSIDE DOWN AT THE BOTTOM OF THE PAGE.

1. What is the name of the tiny particles in matter that vibrate to create sound?

2. Which state of matter does sound travel faster through: solid or gas?

3. What happens to the skin on the drum when you play loud music next to it?

4. What unit do we use to measure the volume of sound?

5. How does a megaphone make your voice louder?

6. What is the range of sound waves that humans can hear in hertz?

7. Why do brown long-eared bats make a high-pitched call?

8. What won't you find in an anechoic chamber?

9. What did Alexander Graham Bell invent that allows us to call people from very far away?

10. What did Robert William Boyle place inside of a vacuum to prove that sound travels through matter?

1) Atoms 2) Solid 3) It vibrates 4) Decibels 5) It focuses the sound waves in one direction 6) 20 to 20,000 Hz 7) To find insects 8) Echoes 9) The telephone 10) A bell

GLOSSARY

dog whistles	**high-pitched whistles used to train dogs**
eardrum	**a thin layer of skin in the ear that vibrates when touched by sound waves**
electronically	**by means of electronic devices**
hallucinations	**the perception of something that isn't there**
invented	**created or made up something new**
Latin	**the language of ancient Rome**
trachea	**the tube that carries air from your mouth to your lungs, also called a windpipe**
transmitting	**moving from one place to another**
vacuum	**a space devoid of matter**
vibrate	**make small, shaking movements**

INDEX